Tales of Intrigue & Plumage

Catherine Arra

FUTURECYCLE PRESS
www.futurecycle.org

Cover design by Brandon V. Bennett; cover photo by David Saylor; interior book design by Diane Kistner; Kepler text and titling

Copyright © 2017 Catherine Arra
All Rights Reserved

Published by FutureCycle Press
Athens, Georgia, USA

ISBN 978-1-942371-30-4

for David

Contents

I

Ashokan	9
Ashokan Eaglets & Dusk	10
Eagle	11
Ode to B3	12
First Flight	14
Nested Light	15
Disavowed	16
Rain & Other Complaints	17
November Noise, 2016	18
My House First	19
No Sanctum	20
Winter Solstice	21
Eagle Dream	22

II

Already This Morning	25
from the bowl like mercy itself	26
Feral	27
Lacuna	28
When the Crows Come	29
Rooting & Rising	30
Seasons & Envy	31
Perennial	32
Rapture	33
Tartaruga	34
The End of Night	35
Lakeside Condo with View of 8th Hole & Sand Traps	36
Ballet of Palms	38

Acknowledgments

I

Ashokan

Another evening
of Catskill rounds & slides.
Both eaglets perched
between nest & fledge.
Rip Van Winkle sleeps
among whispers & Indian bones.

Beauty like this is prayer.

Ashokan Eaglets & Dusk

I'd live among you
in these unsullied hills
wing-swirl thermals with cerulean
lavender & late light coral.

I'd prefer perilous nakedness
a wilderness of chance
give way & all to god-sense
surge, soar, lead.

Better to risk the storm
the fall, a thieving hawk
starve by my own neglect
succumb to the better hunter

than to live without sight from above
heart-space, a parched basin below.

I'd rather die with hunger, that voracious hunger
instinct in my belly.

Eagle

The Cherokee named you
    awâhili

the Cheyenne,
    migisi

the Navajo said,
    atsá

the Munsee,
    awéhleew

the Algonquin pointed & called
    mikiziw

the Lakota,
    anúnkasan.

Sacred power animal, essence yoked in form
    they gathered your feathers for rightful passage & ritual
    made music with your bones.
They danced the Eagle Dance among thundering drums
    carved your image high on totems.

Avian messenger bearing prayers aloft
    you alone traverse realms, link heaven & earth.
Through you they knew
    Great Spirit wings, whispers
    delivers grace.

Ode to B3

In the fluted vase of a loblolly pine
    the nest, a broad, twig-tiered affair
        engineered in crisscross, latched-stick precision
        padded with meadow grass

you were born in late February
    (the 22nd, to be exact, & they named you B3)
a Q-tip, bobble-head hatchling all belly hunger & need after
Mama & Papa labored the days of snow

& more snow
the wind, rain, sleet, heat
fog & fate to deliver you finally
    to the sky.

I've watched the weeks—a webcam addict
never without iPad, iPhone, or far from the desktop—witnessing
the cradled wilderness of your rearing, the modeling of manners

    One never kills needlessly. One never wastes food.
    One never abandons its mate or its young.
    One masters the code of its species
    & is true.

Flexing, perching, preening, clawing—then
    branching & mantling
    balancing grand gestures with weighted grace
you wonder at the sky, the distance you will go
& your powers.

At 12 weeks, a down-mottled, silky black grey
    3 feet long, a 6-foot wingspan
    you're still a baby
miscalculating branches & crashing
dive-bombed bullied by blue jays
    needing your mama's belly feathers
    & long night vigils.

Instinct-driven, exhausted
      you nose-dive, belly-flop the nest bed, splay yourself out
      like a paper kite, side-stretch that right leg, those sexy talons
      beak-set your sight over sticks
      to watch & doze
           awaiting the call.
I whisper...
Take your time, lovely girl, go slow...
to this place you can never return.

You say,
      No, it's simple. I'm an eagle.

Then one morning in late May
      (the 22nd, at 7:11 a.m. to be exact)
a flapping silhouette in rising white light
      you claimed the sky
a blinding starburst of sun & webcam
      quivering in your wake

with me, bereft, gutted
      longing, holding & wanting to hold, unlike
your mama who delivers fresh fish, calls you back to nest
      & watches you eat as you always eat.
      It's simple, yes...

but today
before she departs
you nuzzle her belly, stroke her side feathers
with bowed head.

      Could it be...did you?

Go, B3, go
live between sky & pine
      & with you this wild heart.

First Flight

To hesitate (I know)
    you start, go, stop
    wiggle down, adjust
        spring upright, step-step
            step ahead to the edge
            determined, periscope lookout
                ...shift, side-side
                      side-side to a sudden
                      reverse back squat.

    Desire rides tension between doubt & destiny
        the passage entered or not. (I know)

How I imagined this day for you
    the lift, soar, height & grandeur.
How elegant slicing sky
    becoming like wind.
I imagined the crash too
    a sightless spiral, scraping bark
        broken & never rising again.

    Half do not survive the first year
        unwinged or dead (I know)

but you (hard-wired instinct) go
    a fearless statistic either way.

Nested Light

Baby eagle
earth-brown down
where will you go now
lone hunter, seeker without parent or nest

trading innocence for the kill, losing all
(feathers, eyes, beak)
for steel grey, gold
white tail & crown?

Though I've memorized the patterns
in your ashen underwings, studied the tilt
of your exquisite head, I have
no inches on a door frame, circles in a tree

no compass or sextant, no way
to mark migrations, molting
follow the story of your making
from fledgling to mate.

Tell me, baby eagle
where will you go &
how will I know
if ever I see you again?

In the cleavage of your senses
in nested light, in the place where
you found me
(there) all things take flight.

Disavowed

The white man called you
chicken hawk, varmint
shotgunned, trapped & tortured you
laid a petty bounty on your head.

Tales of mythic proportion damned you:
devil birds kill for sport, snatch sleeping infants
devour salmon, livestock.

& then
DDT, the razing of your habitat
noise, clutter
buckshot lead.
Threats foreign to instinct:
turbines, windmills
electric grids.
How to navigate stolen sky.

For your near extinction
forgive my species.

Spirit suffers at unholy hands
but not by you
Eagle
spreading open
heart first, arms wide
giving your whole being
like fragile earth suspended in chaos
to each new day.

Rain & Other Complaints

Depression is an undertow
she's come to rely on, a steadiness in potential displacement
by which a landscape is balanced, a mood composed.

Take today, another
in a long run on rain; a day for red shoes
& writing on the chalkboard in shocked pastels.

Today, an exercise, a simple shifting of sand particles, practice
for the riptides that will dredge stars & spit earth like an olive pit
past hope that even sleep

will yield a dream, a lover, a Messiah
or the next day when fire envelops
a lush green forest & burns nothing.

November Noise, 2016

A crazed woodpecker attacks the house.
Systematic strikes echo like machine-gun fire
the way disbelief ricochets the brain
hammers the skull, perforates bone
the way ravaged cones scar clapboards
breaking   beauty   form   hope
the way the time of cold caverns begins
& the hard-won, most sacred are trumped.

My House First

Hives nested in clapboards
rise with chimney steps
where years of rain-rotted wood made gateway
to apiary heaven, homeland security
bliss, until lethal rain, jets of sting, convulsive retching
of one, then dozens, sending all
into swarmed confusion, never to know
why this act of terror.

Honey bees ringing the birdbath
said it was hornet genocide
& trembled.

No Sanctum

I.

From the crown of an abandoned shell

the one no one wanted for the gift shop
the seaside memento, its flawed chamber etched
& cracked, a sliver shattered from its spire
cast aside, masked in muddied mulch, forgotten
until excavated, knocked, shaken
knocked again

the young gecko cascades to concrete
with wet sand, stunned still.

II.

One-eyed heron spindle-legs the cloistered courtyard
her haven now, abandoned by the flock, never to mate
navigating her half world, half blind.

III.

Fragile is each thread unwound, unbound
isolated without shape, form, purpose:
twigs in a nest, cells of a hive,
people in democracy divided.

Winter Solstice

In this inky womb

she links the stars
        of all her midnights

weaves a cloak of smoky velvet
        anoints her feet with frankincense.

She awaits her hour of balance
        lighting candles
                for the dead
                        for the living
                              for the light
                                      she cannot see
but feels as
        a passion far too hot
                for those who do not know
                        this swampy darkness
                                  & fear drowning.

Eagle Dream

You came
as thunder
archetypal, like the military war birds
that flew low
terrifying 6-year-old legs
under the porch, trembling.
You came
because I missed you
summoned you
because I haven't yet understood
how to let your wings cover me
let your shadow
guide me
let the delicate turn
of your end feathers lift me
& let go.

II

Already This Morning

A pregnant doe, dozing
in a wooded sun patch
another with two fawns, sprinting.
A rabbit, baby woodchucks
three female turkeys, foraging.

Daybreak chores
orders for cardinals, wood hatches, chickadees
nesting wrens in the petunias.
Layered birdsong
like tumbling voices on a distant playground
the hard staccato of crows above.

Life happened underground
in thawing earth, leafless trees;
a thundering pulse
invited me in
while I consumed human days
deaf & numb
wanting
wanting
always wanting more.

from the bowl like mercy itself.

My resident raven cleans & cooks prey
in the birdbath. Eviscerated mouse intestines
a rubber grey heart, baby bird heads &
feathers float in the broth.
All living things are omnivores, vegans too
no lie. A principle learned in the womb on
Mother's blood; on the playground when
Katie pushes Timmy off the swing & he
loves her forever; when Nancy practices
every day to keep fingers fast against envy for
first-chair flute; when the teacher demotes
her anyway because she refuses to march in
the holiday parade; *I don't march,* she says
don't parade, quits his flute & learns guitar
hugs it close, sings protest songs with Randy
outside the café; when the sorority spurns fat
girls & Randy dies at war anyway; when
the husband can't make the wife mind &
cheats instead; when the boss plays grab-ass
quid pro quo; when they waterboard the guy
83 times; when 900 migrants drown; when no
lives matter except one's own.
My resident raven kills with precision, talons
death in a dirty instant; no cat-mouse games.
All living things are prey, but my raven is
crude like oil, shimmers blue, royal gold in
sunlight, absorbs all color into itself, pins it
down, bleeds it into each penned feather tip
& launches

↑ back to top

Feral

My cat
after waiting winter, sleeping storms
lamenting long March rains
stalks now
reclaiming boundaries, assessing territory lost or gained.

Her days of windowpane longing are tallied in nose prints
until she rolls again in dirt
right to left, left to right, pudge paws compassing her fun.
She is gritty & sexy, creeping through unmown grass
buffing to an onyx sheen.

To have the patience of my cat
who has waited winter & waits now
four paws drawn belly-under
back pitched, tail arrowed, nose aimed
ready
for the unsuspecting ground mole that will reaffirm
the order of things lost in domesticity.

Lacuna

She can hardly bear the clicking
of the classroom heater
the unruly chirping of high schoolers, lunch gossip
or committee cackle.

Impatience peaks with static levels
phone buzz produces a scowl.
Bells cause a rash; fire alarms
race her at a feverish pace.

At the end of the day she is like the dust
flitting on air currents caught under her desk.

Her lover doesn't understand why on weekends she complains
about the radio, cringes at his suggestion to dine
at the Hot Spot Café
exiles the dog porchside to muffle thundering paws.

Saturdays she waits
mornings in bed, blinking at the whisper of leaves
the silkening of grass
startled by the occasional grunt of a tulip.

She shuffles past briars of civilized prattle
jungles of argument
bushwhacks language & tiptoes along ear canals.

She finds the precipice overlooking her lacuna
& dives.
Sensation ends
but for a hum, a rhythm,
& the first
modulations of a voice she needs to hear.

When the Crows Come

When the crows came around
rapacious, squawking
raiding nests of phoebes & finches
discarding debris from scavenger hunts in birdbaths

when she couldn't keep the water free
of slimy black feathers, excrement
& the cardinal couple flew elsewhere to bathe

when she woke at 5 a.m. to blood-cries
of slaughter, cannibalism, she knew
it was time to leave.

Something had died in the walls of her castle
a disease was eating the dahlias

predators knew & were circling
death birds mottled the yard

no housecleaning would do
no remodeling or decorating.

You have to leave when the crows come
& before the vulture.

Rooting & Rising

When I see first growth, older than the nation
oaks edging the Hudson, sycamores arching

Old North Bridge in Concord, evergreens marking
the Oregon Trail

When I stumble over roots like well-worked thighs
follow hunger to trunks, round enough to table a king & his knights

When I study architecture, exquisite as any
cathedral, see how wildlife is sheltered, imagination plays

When I'm dwarfed by the will of centuries growing past complacency
I think about longing & desire

droughts forcing saplings underground, storms ripping away branches
forked lightning to test the center

I think about living, loving, the long reach to God
pray for protection against loggers & the greed of my species.

Seasons & Envy

Sweet friend, so good to see you again:
lilies opening earth with determined fingers
fuzzy crew cuts on newborn phlox
emerald lace on honeysuckle.

Your brooding relative has overstayed his welcome
greedy for your green, ravenous for your milk, but
you remain generous. Rather than face you
he slinks back underground, an icy snake

melting into stony fissures.
He coils into caverns littered with carcasses
of motherless fawns, anxious robins, but
you are forgiving.

You know he will wait there
& you know this too: his waiting, his night.
You know he is unrivaled & abandoned.
You alone are the cocktail that becomes his poison.

Still, you are gracious, would invite him to stay
accommodate him in grassy carpets, daffodils
offer champagne, leave chocolates on his pillow.
How wonderful you are. Or is this your greatest cruelty

knowing he would perish trying?
Am I kinder to simply wish him gone
having known his darkness, picked at his bones
while you vacationed in the Bahamas?

Better I should dream of faraway places, where
he is the alien, an accident of nature, without friends
& not I.

Perennial

Lush are the gardens this year:
rhododendrons plumped pink
azalea bells ringing white jubilee
variegated fern, purple lamium, woodruff
footing baptisia & flax spiking blue
into daybreak, haloed green.

I will not be disappointed if next year's garden
(as I was in last year's) is less.
I will not harbor expectations, make comparisons.

I will live each year like this:
sometimes fertile, festive
other times a mere pass at respectable, & then
drought, blight, ghostly fungi, insects;
a root to crown weeding of what cannot be sustained.

Rapture

Like silver dust in fountains of sudden sun & heat
damselflies shimmer above wet grass
hover alone, in swarms, small gatherings
dawdle with dandelion seeds, helicopter rise & descend
as if with wind, soar on spears of fairy breath, but
oh so intentional, this mating dance
this whimsical right to be.

I watch them commingle, touch
kiss & linger, kiss & spin in whirling eros

starships at warp speed & gone.

Tartaruga

There is no language
in the place the two-hundred-year-old tartaruga knows

alone each day, walled in the palazzo garden
with little or no sunlight, little or no food.

I watch him furrow warm yellow patches of mid-afternoon
& stay, letting his hard green shell heat the chambers of his solitude.

Each day I bring fresh lettuce, he's less frightened. Today he's waiting
his diamond head stretching up, his reptile eyes shining.

How wonderful to be noticed in this wordless world
to be tended to, cared for, to be seen in this singular, ancient garden

in his only shell.

The End of Night

Without a cosmic canopy, breath solitude, sightless sense

Without stars, whitewashed in safety glow
galaxies swallowed in electric auras

Without midnight ink, silver dreams, a way to navigate dusk to dawn
know the difference between shadow & night

Without sleep, lost to glare: nightlight, floodlight, sweeping screaming
motion light, clock light, router, modem, red white blue siren light

we are the monsters under the bed.

Lakeside Condo with View of 8th Hole & Sand Traps

I.

To rise

with sun
see sandhill cranes commune
feed on the green before canopied carts
& pastel shirts descend, dispersing
all in frantic flutter;

witness grand flight
in pairs, flocks, elegant long necks
wings stretched to purpose
high-pitched, rattling calls
of greetings, joy
the choreographed precision in landing;
serenely slow, supine, they mate for life
in red-capped royalty.

See the lone fishers: great white egrets
ibis like stars shimmering in electric dawn
old man-shouldered blue heron long-legging the shoreline.

See the alligator named "Swims in Morning"
launch from marsh grass with submarine stealth
glide the distance of a new day.

Every year grand houses & coral rooftops
multiply, swallow scrub & flora
yet wild things adapt
allow, invite us by grace of being
to look up from civilized rush
to not run them down, bloodied feathers
on concrete where once they fed.

II.

To aim

well, avoid sand traps set on a slant
two oblong trenches like teardrops, designed
to ensnare every boast, proclaimed intention
each practiced swing, competitive chuckle
& then
sandblast a way out; scratchy particles stick to sweat
golf buddies watch, side-glance down
while humiliation is raked smooth.

III.

To pray

like the anhinga after a day of diving
snorkeling wetlands & waterways
snatching the tastiest catch to feed her young.
At dusk, a lone priestess
perched on a rock, storm drain, fence.
Golden neck snakes upward;
bat-like wings glisten, a velvet cape
flung open to dry in air still warm with sun.

Read the divinations in mink-marble-bronze
upon plumage, her back arched now
heart pressed to amber.

Ballet of Palms

To have the resilience of palms
lift, sway, backbend, hula
a streaming mane curling
long necks of wind, then
a ponytail, pigtails, tight French twist
budding flora unfurling, flattening
pedaling up & down
ocean in crescendo, crest, calamitous cascade
or still as moon in lagoon sky.

To be as force & fond desire
supple before disaster.

Acknowledgments

Grateful acknowledgment is made to the editors of the publications in which versions of these poems first appeared.

Cahoodaloodaling: "Tartaruga"
11/9: The Fall of American Democracy: "November Noise, 2016"
First Literary Review-East: "Rain & Other Complaints"
Flash Frontier: "from the bowl like mercy itself."
Nine Mile Magazine: "Ode to B3," "First Flight," "Nested Light"
Nixes Mate Review: "No Sanctum," "My House First"
Peacock Journal: "The End of Night," "Eagle," "Lacuna," "Winter Solstice"
Postcards Poems and Prose: "Ashokan"
Split Rock Review: "Lakeside Condo with View of 8th Hole & Sand Traps"
Upstater: "Ashokan Eaglets & Dusk"

Thanks to my publisher, Diane Kistner, Director at FutureCycle Press.

My gratitude to the steady and soulful Stone Ridge Library writers, Frank Boyer, Bill Fellenberg, Sheila Finan, Fay Loomis, Michael Polcari, Carol Shank, Scott Woods, Jose Sotolongo, Cliff Mallory, and Cecilia Worth. Your insightful feedback and support are invaluable.

Warm thanks to my friends, Beverly Bennett, Linda Harris, Trudi Melamed, Karen Scott, Bret Scott, Elissa Jury, Jim Naccarato, Faye Eichholzer, Rima Walker, Cheryl Rice, and everyone who reads my work, cheers, and shows up at my poetry readings.

Special thanks to David Saylor for allowing the use of his alluring photograph for the cover, and to graphic artist and lifelong friend Brandon Bennett for his amazing cover design.

Big thanks to multitalented editor-writers Cindy Hochman, Michelle Elvy, W. F. Lantry, and C. Wade Bentley for their kind words and generosity of spirit.

And loving gratitude to the man at the center of my life and heart, David Michael Cook.

About FutureCycle Press

FutureCycle Press is dedicated to publishing lasting poetry books, chapbooks, and anthologies in the English language in both print-on-demand and Kindle ebook formats. Founded in 2007 by long-time independent editor/publishers and partners Diane Kistner and Robert S. King, the press incorporated as a nonprofit in 2012. A number of our editors are distinguished poets and writers in their own right, and we have been actively involved in the small press movement going back to the early seventies.

The FutureCycle Poetry Book Prize and honorarium is awarded annually for the best full-length volume of poetry we publish in a calendar year. Introduced in 2013, our Good Works projects are anthologies devoted to issues of universal significance, with all proceeds donated to a related worthy cause. Our Selected Poems series highlights contemporary poets with a substantial body of work to their credit; with this series we strive to resurrect work that has had limited distribution and is now out of print.

We are dedicated to giving all of the authors we publish the care their work deserves, making our catalog of titles the most diverse and distinguished it can be, and paying forward any earnings to fund more great books.

We've learned a few things about independent publishing over the years. We've also evolved a unique, resilient publishing model that allows us to focus mainly on vetting and preserving for posterity poetry collections of exceptional quality without becoming overwhelmed with bookkeeping and mailing, fundraising activities, or taxing editorial and production "bubbles." To find out more about what we are doing, come see us at www.futurecycle.org.

www.ingramcontent.com/pod-product-compliance
Lightning Source LLC
Chambersburg PA
CBHW070453050426
42450CB00012B/3263